The Historians

The Historians

POEMS

Eavan Boland

W. W. NORTON & COMPANY
Independent Publishers Since 1923

For information about permission to reproduce selections from this book,
write to Permissions, W. W. Norton & Company, Inc.,
500 Fifth Avenue, New York, NY 10110

For information about special discounts for bulk purchases, please contact
W. W. Norton Special Sales at specialsales@wwnorton.com or 800-233-4830

Manufacturing by Versa Press
Book design by Marysarah Quinn
Production manager: Lauren Abbate

Library of Congress Cataloging-in-Publication Data
Names: Boland, Eavan, author.
Title: The historians : poems / Eavan Boland.
Description: First edition. | New York, NY : W. W. Norton & Company, [2020]
Identifiers: LCCN 2020017149 | ISBN 9781324006879 (hardcover) |
ISBN 9781324006886 (epub)
Subjects: LCGFT: Poetry.
Classification: LCC PR6052.O35 H57 2020 | DDC 821/.914—dc23
LC record available at https://lccn.loc.gov/2020017149

W. W. Norton & Company, Inc., 500 Fifth Avenue, New York, N.Y. 10110
www.wwnorton.com

W. W. Norton & Company Ltd., 15 Carlisle Street, London W1D 3BS

1 2 3 4 5 6 7 8 9 0

For Ella, Jack, Julia, and Cian.

Contents

III

MARGIN

IV

OUR FUTURE WILL BECOME
THE PAST OF OTHER WOMEN

I

THE HISTORIANS

I

THE FIRE GILDER

She loved silver, she loved gold,
my mother. She spoke about the influence
of metals, the congruence of atoms,
the art classes where she learned
these things: *think of it*
she would say as she told me
to gild any surface a master craftsman
had to meld gold with mercury,
had to heat both so one was volatile,
one was not
and to do it right
had to separate them and then
burn, burn, burn mercury
until it fled and left behind
a skin of light. *The only thing,* she added—
but what came after that I forgot.

What she spent a lifetime forgetting
could be my subject:
the fenced-in small towns of Leinster,

the coastal villages where the language
of the sea was handed on,
phrases bruised by storms,
by shipwrecks. But isn't.
My subject is the part wishing plays in
the way villages are made
to vanish, in the way I learned
to separate memory from knowledge,
so one was volatile, one was not
and how I started writing,
burning light,
building heat until all at once
I was the fire gilder
ready to lay radiance down,
ready to decorate *it happened*
with *it never did* when
all at once I remember what it was
she said: *the only thing is*
it is extremely dangerous.

II

EPITHALAMION

A migrant poem
that became our neighbor:
every rhyme of it,
every steep incline
of syntax
rooted in colony,
its music made
for marriages,
but only those
to which it could be
ode and emissary.
Epithalamion: meaning
a song for a bride,
for a bridegroom,
to ease them into praise,
into ceremony as
they could never be—
that wife and husband
I will never find

who died outside
these lines.
        The shawl
of earth with its shreds
of ditch flowers
that wrapped their bones
was composed
in an Irish anywhere
that let too little light in
for anyone to see.
All we know is
the winds that blew in from
our stolen ocean
brought salt.
They provided the wounds.

III

THE BAROGRAPH

I found it on the quays,
a rectangle of wood,
a barograph, its pen arm inking paper.

I brought it home to be
a register of winds,
of rising pressure,

able to write the barometric fate
of our dailyness
back in a world where

windblown book carts by the river
promised wild words
but obeyed the censor.

Banks in College Green
recorded pounds in ledgers,
pennies in the margin.

Meanwhile we were walking
the old roads,
the elms dying over us. Then

another time came: our screens
filled with supper funerals
we watched in silence,

each of us thinking
what was changed
was changed forever. Yet

every day the page was inked,
the pen still ready to be
what it had always been:

scribe of our Irish climate,
knowing no suffering, just
the hours as they opened, closed,

opened. Unable to understand events,
only the weather
in which they happened.

IV

THE LIGHT WE LOST

Repeat the word *sainthood* and we are
in an old Ireland,
in a time warp of tallow—

candle smoke rising towards
the porcelain
yellow faces of the sanctified.

I look up. Painted on glass
inside the algebras
of windows spaces

they look down: savage azures
keeping out the light of
a small country.

V

THE LAMPLIGHTER

In the old lithographs
and situational drawings
in which dusk appears
as a series

of outcomes and intrusions,
you will see him
standing up to night,
holding up a long pole,

a wick at one end,
sizing up his task.
You will recognize
the lamplighter

who once was a small
lawmaker re-drawing street
corners and neighborhoods
in our city

after midnight
with his nightly care
and his bright line. After midnight
I stare at the page.

How often I long to lift
my words high. How
often nothing is raised
and nothing brightens.

I read once
that when he heard
loud whispers and laughter
in alleys and hidden doorways

followed by
the silence of illicit kisses
he would not stop
he would pass on

to other streets
where light was needed.
Leaving behind him
the gift of shadows.

VI

ANONYMOUS

She was a closed book,
a near relative.
Almost the same age
as the century.
I once heard
she carried messages,
communications, worn-
out documents,
ferrying revolt
to the far corners
of Haddington Road
and O'Connell Street.

On cold nights
when mist rolls in
from the ocean
somewhere near Clontarf
I think I see her strolling,
holding on
to a folded message,

a dispatch order.
Then I ask myself,
what is it I know?
The evening mist unfolds.
It is empty. That
is history. This
is only poetry.

VII

EVICTION

Back from Dublin, my grandmother
finds an eviction notice on her door.
Now she is in court for rent arrears.
The lawyers are amused.
These are the Petty Sessions,
this is Drogheda, this is the Bank Holiday.
Their comments fill a column in the newspaper.
Was the notice well served?
Was it served at all?
Is she a weekly or a monthly tenant?
In which one of the plaintiffs' rent books
is she registered?
The case comes to an end, is dismissed.
Leaving behind the autumn evening.
Leaving behind the room she entered.
Leaving behind the reason I have always
resisted history.
A woman leaves a courtroom in tears.
A nation is rising to the light.
History notes the second not the first.

Nor does it know the answer as to why
on a winter evening
in a modern Ireland
I linger over the page of the *Drogheda
Argus and Leinster Journal*, 1904,
knowing as I do that my attention has
no agency, none at all. Nor my rage.

VIII

THE HISTORIANS

Say the word *history*: I see
your mother, mine.
The light sober, the summer well over,
an east wind dandling leaves, rain stirring at the kerb.

Their hands are full of words.
One of them holds your father's journal with its note
written on the day you were born.
The other my small rhymed scratchings, my fervent letters.
Before the poem ends
they will have burned them all.

Now say the word again. Summon
our island: a story that needed to be told—
the patriots still bleeding in the lithographs
when we were born. Those who wrote that story
labored to own it.

But these are women we loved.
Record-keepers with a different task.
To stop memory becoming history.
To stop words healing what should not be healed.

It is cold. The light is going.
They kneel now behind their greenhouses,
beneath whichever tree is theirs.

The leaves shift down.
Each of them puts a match to the paper. Then
they put their hands close to the flame.
They feel the first bite of the wind.
They lace their pages with fire. I finish writing.

II

HOW WE WERE TRANSFIGURED

FOR A POET WHO DIED YOUNG

Even now I see myself there
your book propped on the kitchen table.

When I closed it your poems would not stay put.
They roamed the house. They saw my children sleeping.
They stared out the window.

They looked into
the sly double vowels of Ursa Major or Lyra.
They knew the stars inside were tired of signifying

wheat and old beasts. They understood
these were once women
who wanted earthliness,

the sort that understood a circle or the origin
of stoneware or a blueness
they could never see at night.

You died young. Your words helped me live.
I was younger then. Your ghost is still young.
Is still dead.

Your words disturbed my earth. They changed my mind.
Whatever a dead poet could have I wish for you.
But a living woman

is what you should have been. So many years later
forgive the fact my words unlike yours
offer little comfort and less peace.

RAIN

I was born in a place where rain
is second nature, where a hooded coat,
    ready on the hook,
        was never out of reach. Nor
do I believe like Plato, or even
his late revisionists, that landscape
  is the corporeal purpose
        of our minds. I always knew
rain was a dialect I could listen to
on a winter night: its sibilance.
    Even now, on a wet evening,
        I watch as twilight comes
to the old graveyard above the main
road of our village and I am glad for
    whoever lies there that this
        elemental companion has not,
and never will, abandon them.

·

HOW WE WERE TRANSFIGURED

Now when darkness starts
                in mid-afternoon,
when evening shows an unwelcome
                half-sliced winter moon
                I remember days
when I never thought twice about
                what was farther off
                from the four walls of our
                house, from the hills
above it, from our infant daughters sleeping
                in it or what lay
                in wait for us on the Irish Sea
                as darkness moved up
and away and we slept late oblivious
                to the rain's drizzle,
                the tap and flicker of it,
                to what was coming
silently, insistently, to render
                our lives visible to us again:

light the builder,
light the maker, fitter of roofs to gutters,
of the tree's root
to the tree's height,
of earth to sky:
assembler of openings at
the river's mouth and the mind's eye.

THIS GARDEN

Awake late at night what I see is
faces, faces, their radiance. And realize
I will never see them again. Then

I come to this place, to this garden:
A stretch of grass, fog-wet at dawn
reaching past hutch wire, sweet pea,

the chiming of small apples falling, still
falling by which time it will be twilight.
At the end of the path is a gate

creaking open on flickering
teatime windows and the Wicklow hills,
and beyond their blueness the horizon

of a new nation: and here at least,
those mean consonants, those actors of injury—
Moneta, Mnemosyne—are nowhere to be seen.

Where I stand there is no *then* or *once.*
It is September. Crab apples are littered
in the grass, their skin torn by wild beaks.

It is September. In another hour, I will be born.
Until then I cannot be alive.
Until then I have no need to remember.

BE

If I think of it
what I see are hills—
kinetic, never still
shadows building
necessary blues
to make dusk.

If I think of it,
it is already autumn,
whitethorn trees
with their steeped-
in-tannin leaves
disappearing in
the frame of my window.

If I think of it
what I see are
the first days of spring,
snowdrops just barely

visible, but how
they came to be there
I will never know.

All I know is
as the light went my
infant daughters
were asleep in it,
brightness arcing towards
a cambered distance.

All I know is
some days
should simply be.
Not be remembered.

LOST

Things I thought could be misplaced—

a notebook, a favorite pen—
but not

that quick conversation beside the hedge
on a summer day

in July
years ago. Whose smile is that?

Who am I answering the door to
on an airy morning,

the plants everywhere
blooming?

How do I connect the bent head
with that hand
cutting roses?

I find my pen behind the curtain
with my notebook.

I should have taken more care.

WITHOUT END

When I woke that morning
I wondered whether
the start and finish of
the legend, or at least
the fraction of it
that was in my mind,
was accurate.

Then Jack and Ella
came to play, finding
things to throw and dig up
in our garden, whatever two
years old could manage or
four make use of.

A mythic Irish king,
restless and bored
with his storytellers,
featured in it.
I remember that.
And that he banished them.

It was time now
for Julia, only one
year of age, to arrive.

What was it settled him?
What brought him back
to the climb and balance
and advance of narrative?

Our grandchildren
stand in the same place
their mothers, our daughters,
once did. The same light
mapped onto their gestures,
their faces. The same lilac
bending towards them.

I remembered then what
it was restored him:
he found at last
the one storyteller
with the one story
that had no ending.

THREE CRAFTS

The spindle was hammered into the stock of the wheel.
The legs were turned and smoothed
and propped up the spinning motion

which made a small, odd music—more a whirring, really—
enough to cover up the sound
a tree makes on a summer night.

The frame that was woven under the currach
was wood and canvas. It was made
out of willow or sometimes hazel and was ready

for the waters of the western seaboard,
a world away from how those same branches
once dragged a quiet river in Lucan.

On wild nights when trees are getting ready
to become memories of themselves
no one will remember I remember

stumbling into this art when I was young.
How often I wrote late at night hoping
as window latches broke loose and the wind

rose and undid all the leaves that what I wrote
might be capable of learning from
an ocean cadence. Its fall, its rise and fall.

TRANSLATING THE WORD *HOME*

A small city disappears in
the near-sighted dusk of a coastal winter.
Someone is walking home as I once did.
Someone is thinking as I did once:
this is their neighborhood, their consolation.

Once I thought words could describe this.
Now I reach for the sable brush
my mother once used, lifting it clear
from the jar of turpentine
it hasn't steeped in for fifty years.

An arm bent. Carmine and magenta.
Alizarine. Cobalt. Yellow ochre.
She is painting a Connemara summer:
a riddle of ocean light, a gannet
riding a wave, a creel of mackerel

The canvas stretched out and ready
to be tacked to the frame, made tight,
primed with animal glues and linseed,
measuring three by two, more or less.
The gesso put on with a wide brush.

An English fog outside the window.
West of Ireland distances on canvas.
My mother settling the palette to her left,
putting her thumb in the opening,
reaching for the brush in its jar.

What would I do if I found it now?
That sable brush that began its journey
on the back of a weasel at the center
of a Siberian wood and then migrated
from there to the wing of a cormorant

laced with cold Atlantic water.
I would use it, I am sure of this,
to unsay my own evening, or at least
those parts of it that could be unsaid.
Granite. Ocean grit. Distance.

I would dip the sable in *shadow*
until a winter evening came in view,
its outlined windows reappearing
on a road with someone walking home,
who might be me, inhaling peat smoke.

Then open a stitched and bound sketchbook
and dip the brush again in *azure*,
lowering the tip of it in *window*
and *yellow light* and then wash
the whole watercolor block with *home*.

III

MARGIN

BROKEN

I almost never dream. When I do
I hardly ever remember what I dreamed.

Sentient blues, knotted together pieces
of a beautiful otherness, are usually
shifted back at dawn to be shadows.

This was different. I was walking
down to the river as I often did.
To right and left of me old patriots,
their mouths stuffed with bronze,
their words falling onto winter plinths.

The way that dreams are, this was:
my hands at first skin, then linen.
Their hands cast in metal, a set color.

I reached the Liffey, passing crowds,
cars, sirens, my own words falling

into an old question: *Ireland*
how could I ever have loved you
if I never believed you?

A woman's head fell into the river.
A parapet fanned the surface. Then
a windowsill and a caved-in roof
wavered up slowly through molecules
of worn-out light and city grime.

I looked down and saw my face there.
Underwater, broken. Then I woke.

SO FAR AWAY

In the Blackwater Valley
beneath the Knockmealdowns
a man was singing
about the death of another man.

I could hear thrushes and a river.
Wings beating over walls of fuchsia.
The back and forth
freshwater wash over stones.

That was a moment when
I could have said I am
another self: an agent able
to cast away what had happened

so moor grass and pin moss
could reclaim a landscape
that had existed
before suffering became a habit.

I was listening to a song
sending its echo into the evening,
hearing those words
as they insisted

a man with no time left for history
and nothing but a tune
to convey its absence,
died for this. He died for this.

TWO WATERS

I was born between two waters:

Vikings rode the Liffey.
They drowned books.
They plundered monasteries.
They sealed our future
with their long ships.
But rivers heal.

What could heal
this other water,
this Irish Sea,
soured by emigrant tears?

On winter mornings,
I watch as
its rain-dashed waves
break on granite,
warning record-keepers

not to write down
an old grief:

As if the sea
could remember it.
Or the future be able to recite it.

THE BREAK-UP OF A LIBRARY
IN AN ANGLO-IRISH HOUSE
IN WEXFORD: 1964

If you arrive by a side road
opening out and ending in a gate
made from an alphabet of iron animals

and start up an elm-lined avenue
leading to the house
you will enter and see

books for sale by the window,
sleeved in leather
holding in treatises on reason.

As you leave say to yourself
the word *habitat:*
a natural home or environment

of an animal or plant—
then watch the elms march towards
the day they will lose theirs

with the metal animals who have never,
no matter what sun rose or set,
had one and reflect

the end of empire is and will always be
not sedition nor the whisper
of conspiracy but that

slipper chair in the hallway
that has lost the name
no one will call it by again.

STATUE 2016

Stephen's Green. A half torso.
Her head and shoulders framed
by the coarse flowers of the boxwood shrub.

I was young here. In those years
night came quickly down on my neighborhood.

My children slept, worn out by play.
When I lit the lamp in the corner
my hands were made of light.

That reason and faith are at odds
(and will always be) I accept.
Also that this season cannot matter now
to the woman raised above me on a plinth.

A scalding alloy of tin and copper once
rinsed everything out of her head.
Molten bronze poured away her name

and whatever else of memory
might have been there, even
the apple blossoms of her native Magherlow:

all of it flensed off to make this fixed look.
To make it seem set. To make it look necessary.
I will never be convinced.

COMPLICIT

When we were young we praised Saint Brigid's Day
as if we gave her credit for
the end of our island winter.

I used to think it was our innocence.
Now I think we were the Angelus
I heard when I was still at boarding school,

listening at the window, the music of a bell
acting on the air, collecting
lilac, ozone, light from the water—

each element eliciting meaning
from the other, each arriving at
my windowsill. Inseparable. Complicit.

THREE WAYS IN WHICH
POEMS FAIL

SCRIBE

Under an arc of stars,
on a cold night, in a moral dark,
his hand is straying from

the vowels he has flayed
all afternoon with azurite.
The poem he begins in the margin

does not know how to say
the striking distance the ships
are within nor the word *Viking*.

The monk moves his pen
from the image to the edge,
from the icon to the margin.

He writes: *as the harbor
is welcome to the sailor
So is the last line to the scribe.*

Virgil in the *Georgics* was the first
or so he said
to lead the Muses
into the river shadows of Lombardy.

I am reading how
this Latinate prince of new beginnings
introduced his high-toned fictions
to stripped willows,
deeper water.

Outside my window
January dark
brings ocean salt, grit and seeds
to another freezing Irish dawn.

I wonder now if he ever wept
as he let them wander,
if he doubted whether
they could learn to understand an origin.

I remember how I longed
to find the plenitude and accuracy needed
to bring words home,
to winter hills, fogged-away stars,
children's faces fading into sleep.

Now I wonder
if it was enough.
                    Enough Virgil,
even at this distance, to make us weep?

Silence was a story, I thought,
on its own and all to itself. Then
the storm came. It came to us
with bulletins, forecasts, data,
each coordinate warning us
the doors of the ocean were open
to a wind with an appetite
for roadside bins, roofs,
treetops, the painted henhouse
made to stop foxes that blew away
as lightly as the hat the woman failed
to hold on to as she walked past
Stephen's Green, a sudden gust
catching it: wood and wire mesh
that had once sheltered hands
as they warmed to new eggs
on a winter morning now
stirred into flight over fences
and scoured grass.

                          Hours earlier
it was quiet in the garden.
The pigeons we were used to
hearing all morning were all gone.
Outside the window it seemed

a space had opened, an emptiness.
I knew then what I wanted
to write was not storms
or wet air, it was something
else: it was metaphor and yet
what was made for language
when language cannot carry
meaning failed here. Instead
I learned in the hushed garden
before the wind rose what
I needed to know. Silence told the story.

MARGIN

Yesterday I read about the hawk moth,
common enough in the west
and south of this island—

how it can slow its brain down
at the end of the day so as to see better
in failing light.

Today I waited for the last April cloudiness
to turn dark.

I walked out in our neighborhood as hills
slipped into the horizon.

How will we see inside it,
our own dusk?

Flags rising. Memories failing.
No one left to say who those
men in the photograph are.

Old quarrels clothed in a hundred years of heat,
now shivering in the cold.

I walked on past lighted windows,
drawn curtains.

It was colder now and the intimate unsettled colors
showed me up, a transient, a woman
dressed for warmth,

telling the island to myself, as I always have,
so as to see it more clearly:

not the land of fevers and injuries. But the region
I found for myself,
described for myself in my own language,

so I could stand if only for one moment,
on its margin.